GREAT SCHOLARS QUOTES

GREAT SCHOLARS QUOTES

S. KRISHNA SAI TEJA

Made with ❤ on the Notion Press Platform
www.notionpress.com

Contents

Foreword

Preface

The best brains of the nation may be found on the last benches of the classroom.

"Learn from yesterday, live for today, hope for tomorrow. The important thing is not to stop questioning."

"He who can no longer pause to wonder and stand rapt in awe, is as good as dead; his eyes are closed."

"A happy man is too satisfied with the present to dwell too much on the future."

Luxury and Lies have huge maintenance costs. But Truth and Simplicity are self-maintained without any cost.

"Dream, dream, dream. Dreams transform into thoughts and thoughts result in action."

"To succeed in your mission, you must have single-minded devotion to your goal."

"If you fail, never give up because Fail means "First Attempt In Learning".

"Creativity is seeing the same thing but thinking differently."

"Failure will never overtake me if my determination to succeed is strong enough."

Acknowledgements

"Courage, sacrifice, determination, commitment, toughness, heart, talent, guts. That's what little girls are made of."

"We must have the courage to dare and endure."

"Victory or defeat is not important, but the fight itself is everything."

“Thinking should become your capital asset, no matter whatever ups and downs you come across in your life.”

“When our signature changes to autograph, this marks the Success.”

Small aim is a crime; have great aim.

Science is a beautiful gift to humanity; we should not distort it.

We should not give up and we should not allow the problem to defeat us.

If we are not free, no one will respect us.

Poetry comes from the highest happiness or the deepest sorrow.

Prologue

"You have to dream before your dreams can come true."

"Without your involvement, you can't succeed. With your involvement, you can't fail."

"In this world, fear has no place. Only strength respects strength."

"My message, especially to young people is to have the courage to think differently, courage to invent, to travel the unexplored path, courage to discover the impossible and to conquer the problems and succeed. These are great qualities that they must work towards. This is my message to the young people."

"Look at the sky. We are not alone. The whole universe is friendly to us and conspires only to give the best to those who dream and work.

"Success is when your Signature changes to Autograph."

"This is my belief that through difficulties and problems God gives us the opportunity to grow. So when your hopes and dreams and goals are dashed, search among the wreckage, you may find a golden opportunity hidden in the ruins."

"It means, people who are in high and responsible positions if they go against righteousness, righteousness itself will get transformed into a destroyer."

"Science is a beautiful gift to humanity; we should not distort it."

"To succeed in your mission, you must have single-minded devotion to your goal."

Chapter1

"Thinking should become your capital asset, no matter whatever ups and downs you come across in your life."

"Never stop fighting until you arrive at your destined place — that is, the unique you. Have an aim in life, continuously acquire knowledge, work hard, and have the perseverance to realize the great life."

"Educationists should build the capacities of the spirit of inquiry, creativity, entrepreneurial and moral leadership among students and become their role model"

"If you fail, never give up because FAIL means "First Attempt In Learning".

"Dream, dream, dream. Dreams transform into thoughts and thoughts result in action."

"We should not give up and we should not allow the problem to defeat us."

"It Is Very Easy To Defeat Someone, But It Is Very Hard To Win Someone."

"Unless India Stands Up to the World, No one Will Respect Us. In this World, Fear has no Place. Only Strength Respects Strength."

"Be more dedicated to making solid achievements than in running after swift but synthetic happiness."

"Small aim is a crime."

Chapter2

"Courage, sacrifice, determination, commitment, toughness, heart, talent, guts. That's what little girls are made of."

"We must have the courage to dare and endure."

"Victory or defeat is not important, but the fight itself is everything."

"All Birds find shelter during a rain. But Eagle avoids rain by flying above the clouds."

"Don't take rest after your first victory because if you fail in second, more lips are waiting to say that your first victory was just luck."

"Great dreams of great dreamers are always transcended."

"Teaching is a very noble profession that shapes the character, caliber, and future of an individual. If the people remember me as a good teacher, that will be the biggest honour for me."

"To become 'unique,' the challenge is to fight the hardest battle which anyone can imagine until you reach your destination."

"My view is that at a younger age your optimism is more and you have more imagination etc. You have less bias."

"To preserve my brains I want food and this is now my first consideration. Any sympathetic letter from you will be helpful to me here to get a scholarship..."

Chapter3

"When learning is purposeful, creativity blossoms. When creativity blossoms, thinking emanates. When thinking emanates, knowledge is fully lit. When knowledge is lit, economy flourishes."

"Let us sacrifice our today so that our children can have a better tomorrow."

"Let me define a leader. He must have vision and passion and not be afraid of any problem. Instead, he should know how to defeat it. Most importantly, he must work with integrity."

"Where there is righteousness in the heart, there is harmony in the house; when there is harmony in the house, there is order in the nation; when there is order in the nation, there is peace in the world."

"Life is a difficult game. You can win it only by retaining your birthright to be a person."

"You see, God helps only people who work hard. That principle is very clear."

"Man needs his difficulties because they are necessary to enjoy success."

"You can't change your future but you can change your habits and surely your habits will change your future."

"The best brains of the nation may be found on the last benches of the classroom."

"No sanction can stand against ignited minds."

Chapter4

"No religion has mandated killing others as a requirement for its sustenance or promotion."

"End is not the end, in fact END means "Effort Never Dies" — If you get No as an answer, remember NO means "Next Opportunity". So let's be positive."

"Be active! Take on responsibility! Work for the things you believe in. If you do not, you are surrendering your fate to others."

"When the problem arises — become the captain of the problem and defeat it"

"Before God trusts you with success, you have to prove yourself humble enough to handle the big prize"

"If a country is to be corruption free and become a nation of beautiful minds, I strongly feel there are three key societal members who can make a difference. They are the father, the mother and the teacher."

"Don't read success stories, you will only get a message. Read failure stories, you will get some ideas to get success."

"When we tackle obstacles, we find hidden reserves of courage and resilience we did not know we had. And it is only when we are faced with failure do we realise that these resources were always there within us. We only need to find them and move on with our lives."

"Love your job but don't love your company, because you may not know when your company stops loving you."

"While children are struggling to be unique, the world around them is trying all means to make them look like everybody else."

Chapter5

"You have to dream before the dream comes true.

"The bird is powered by its own life and by its motivation."

"One best book is equal to a hundred good friends, but one good friend is equal to a library."

"We Should not give up and we should not allow the problem to defeat us."

"All of us do not have equal talent. But, all of us have an equal opportunity to develop our talents."

"Thinking is the capital, an enterprise is a way, and hard work is the solution."

"The essence of a happy life and a peaceful society lies in one sentence – What can I Give?"

"Confidence and hard work is the best medicine to kill the disease called failure. it will make you a successful person."

"Life is a difficult game. You can win it only by retaining your birthright to be a person."

"I am not a Handsome guy, but I can give my hand-to-some one who needs help. beauty is in the heart not in the face."

Chapter6

"You cannot change your future, but you can change your habits, and surely your habits will change your future."

"LIFE and TIME are the world's best Teachers. Life teaches us to make good use of TIME and TIME teaches us the value of LIFE."

"Love Your Job but don't love your company, because you may not know when your company stops loving you."

"Knowledge with action converts adversity into prosperity."

"Great dreams of great dreamers are always transcended."

"We have no ability to be equal to all have opportunities equal to their ability lane."

"Success is when your signature turns into your autograph."

"Man needs difficulties because to enjoy the success that they need to."

"Excellence is a continuous process and not an accident."

"Look at the sky. we are not alone. The whole universe is friendly to us and conspires only to give the best to those who dream and work."

Chapter7

"Each work has to pass through these stages: ridicule, opposition, and then acceptance. Those who think ahead of their time are sure to be misunderstood."

"They alone live, who live for others."

"The whole life is a succession of dreams. My ambition is to be a conscious dreamer, that is all."

"Are great things ever done smoothly? Time, patience, and indomitable will must show."

"The children of today will make the India of tomorrow. The way we bring them up will determine the future of the country."

"Only through right education can a better order of society be built up."

"Two things are infinite: the universe and human stupidity; and I'm not sure about the universe."

"There are only two ways to live your life. One is as though nothing is a miracle. The other is as though everything is a miracle."

"Try not to become a man of success. Rather become a man of value."

"It is not that I'm so smart. But I stay with the questions much longer."

9 798890 021762

Printed by Libri Plureos GmbH in Hamburg,
Germany